WHO IS JESUS?

Jesus is the name at the heart of the Christian faith. A village carpenter who became a preacher, he called people to listen to his teaching and follow his example. In the two thousand years since he walked this earth, he has inspired millions of people around the world.

Christina Goodings
Illustrated by Maria Royse

LION
CHILDREN'S

Text by Christina Goodings
Illustrations copyright © 2016 Maria Royse
This edition copyright © 2016 Lion Hudson

Published by Lion Children's Books
an imprint of
Lion Hudson plc
Wilkinson House, Jordan Hill Road,
Oxford OX2 8DR, England
www.lionhudson.com/lionchildrens

ISBN 978 0 7459 6596 3

First edition 2016

Acknowledgments
Bible extracts are taken or adapted from the Good News Bible © 1994 published by the Bible Societies/HarperCollins Publishers Ltd UK, Good News Bible© American Bible Society 1966, 1971, 1976, 1992.
Used with permission.

A catalogue record for this book is available from the British Library
Printed and bound in Malaysia, January 2016, LH18

Contents

The Time of Jesus

Two thousand years ago, the Romans were a world superpower. From their great city of Rome they ruled many of the lands around the Mediterranean Sea.

Among the peoples they had defeated were the Jews. The Jews treasured ancient stories of their nation's very beginning. They believed that God had chosen them to be a people apart, one who would show God's love and mercy to all the world.

They also believed that God had promised them the ancient land of Canaan. They remembered how, about a thousand years earlier, their great king, David, had ruled it as one kingdom.

In the centuries since David, first one empire and then another had made the Jews their subjects. Over the years wise prophets had spoken words of hope: that one day God would send another king like David. He would set up a new kingdom – one that would never end.

The Jewish people looked forward to the coming of this messiah, the Christ.

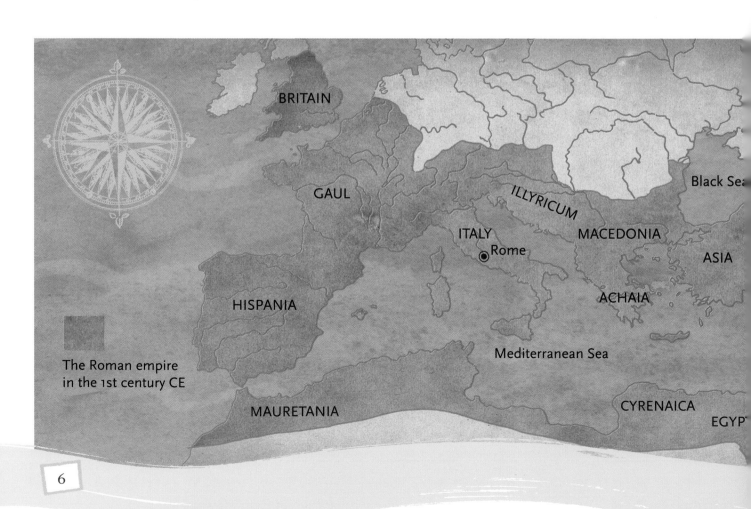

The Roman empire in the 1st century CE

BRITAIN

GAUL

ILLYRICUM

ITALY
Rome

MACEDONIA

Black Sea

ASIA

ACHAIA

HISPANIA

Mediterranean Sea

MAURETANIA

CYRENAICA

EGYPT

David was a shepherd boy. One day, his father sent him to take some food to his brothers, who were fighting the Philistines.

The Philistine champion, Goliath, challenged the army to a duel. Everyone else was too afraid, but with God's help, and a sling and a stone, David defeated the giant.

David went on to become king. He was a good musician and wrote many songs of praise to God – these are known as the Psalms.

SYRIA

Roman troops policed the land of Jesus.

Jerusalem

"David's royal family is like a tree that has been cut down; but just as new branches sprout from a stump, so a new king will arise from David's descendants.

"He will know what pleases God and will show respect by his obedience to God's will.

"He will judge the poor fairly and defend the rights of the helpless.

"Even wild animals will be at peace in his kingdom."

Words of the prophet Isaiah, from Isaiah 11

Growing Up in Nazareth

Jesus grew up in a town called Nazareth, in the region of Galilee.

At home

His mother Mary would have been in charge of the household. There was so much to do each day.

cooking and baking

fetching water

growing vegetables

chisel

Mary was married to Joseph, who was a carpenter. From when he was very young, Jesus would have been taught the trade.

Carpenters used a variety of tools to make household items and farming implements.

At school

Jesus would have gone to school like the other boys. The teacher – the rabbi – taught the boys to read and write. Everything the Jews believed about themselves and their God was in their treasured writings, the Scriptures. The boys had to learn both to read and to understand them.

The boys would have practised their writing on wooden tablets inlaid with wax.

At the synagogue

The Jewish people believed that, from the beginning of time, God had ruled that every seventh day should be a day of rest. This sabbath was a day when people went to the synagogue. There they heard the words of the Scriptures read aloud. The rabbi taught them what it meant to live as God wanted, obeying God's laws.

The ark, where the scrolls were kept.

The Scriptures were written on scrolls.

The menorah, the seven-branched lampstand.

lectern

Men took turns reading the Scriptures. Then the rabbi would explain the meaning of the ancient words.

A Festival in Jerusalem

In the time of Jesus, a boy was considered a young man at the age of twelve.

So it was that the twelve-year-old Jesus was allowed to join other people from Nazareth for the annual trip to the big city of Jerusalem.

At the Temple there they celebrated the most important of all the Jewish festivals: Passover.

Passover

According to the ancient writings, the Jewish people had once been slaves in Egypt. God chose a man named Moses to lead them to the land of Canaan and to freedom. The festival of Passover celebrated their escape.

By the time of Jesus, part of the festival was to worship at the Temple in Jerusalem. Another part was a special festival meal eaten in the company of family and friends.

People shared bread and wine. They remembered the agreement God had made with their people – the covenant. If they obeyed God's commandments, they would be God's people, and God would bless them.

Exodus 12

bread

herb salad

wine cup

wine jug

Jesus in the Temple

When the Passover celebrations were over, the people of Nazareth set off for home.

They had been walking for a whole day before Mary and Joseph noticed Jesus was not with them.

Frantic with worry, they went back to Jerusalem. After three days they found Jesus in the Temple. He was talking with the rabbis – about the Scriptures and what it meant to live in obedience to God.

"Why were you worried?" Jesus asked his mother. "Didn't you know I would be in my Father's house?"

Then he returned home and grew up an obedient son.

Luke 2

In the Temple, Jesus was listening to the rabbis and asking them questions. They were amazed at his intelligent answers.

The Temple building was used for both worship and teaching.

Temple helper

rabbi

Temple priest

Mary and Joseph spot Jesus.

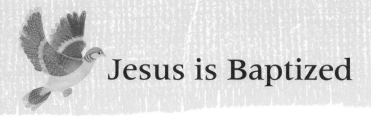

Jesus is Baptized

"Jesus? He's the son of Joseph the carpenter, isn't he?"

That's what everyone in Nazareth would have said about the young man. Jesus was just one of the young working men.

His cousin John was more famous. John had become a preacher. He looked the part of a prophet of olden times, with his uncut hair and rough brown cloak. He lived out in the wild country and foraged for his food.

Even so, people flocked to hear him.

"Get ready for God to come among you," he warned. "Turn from your wicked ways.

"Being selfish, lying, cheating… that's not what God wants.

"If you really want to make a new start, show you're serious: I'll baptize you in the River Jordan."

Matthew 3

John the Baptist

soldiers

tax collector

villagers

Jesus' baptism

One day, Jesus came and asked to be baptized. John was astonished.

"You don't need to," he said. "You haven't ever done anything bad."

"It's important that I do get baptized," Jesus replied. He wanted to show he was starting something new.

As John lifted Jesus out of the water, he saw a dove flutter down and land on Jesus' head. "It's… like God's Holy Spirit," John thought. Then he heard God speaking to Jesus:

"You are my own dear Son. I am pleased with you."

Luke 3

In the wilderness

After he was baptized, Jesus went off alone into the wild country. For forty days he ate nothing. He simply thought and prayed about all that lay ahead. The stories of Jesus say the Devil came to tempt him away from being a preacher, but Jesus knew the Scriptures well. From them he knew what he must do to obey God.

Luke 4

In the wild country, Jesus was all alone with God – and the wild animals.

fox

snake   lizard

13

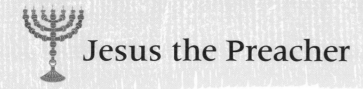
Jesus became a preacher. All over the region of Galilee people flocked to listen.

Goodbye Nazareth

One day, Jesus went home to Nazareth. He was asked to do the reading for the day. Someone handed him the scroll.

He read from the book of the prophet Isaiah:

"God's Spirit is with me.
He has chosen me to bring
good news to the poor,
to set free those who are
in prison or being treated
unfairly,
to bring healing to those
in need,
and to tell everyone that
the time has come
when the Lord will save
his people."

He went and sat down before saying, "Today, these words have come true."

The people of Nazareth were furious. They didn't believe their local boy was a prophet, let alone the messiah. They threw him out of town.

Luke 4

All Jewish men were supposed to take part in reading the Scriptures. Men sat on benches on one side of the synagogue, and women and children sat on the other.

To Capcrnaum

Jesus left Nazareth and went to live in the town of Capernaum, on the shore of Lake Galilee.

He preached in the synagogue on the sabbath, and afterwards was welcomed back to dinner by a fisherman named Simon. (Jesus was later to give him the nickname "Peter", meaning "rock".)

Peter's mother-in-law was unwell. Jesus healed her just by speaking. In no time at all the news spread: Jesus could work miracles!

Luke 4

The kind of fishing boats Jesus' friends would have used had a sail and a steering oar. They would have only just been big enough to carry Jesus and his twelve disciples.

Once healed, Peter's mother-in-law began to attend to Jesus and his friends' needs.

Jesus and His Disciples

Jesus' message was very clear.

"The time is right," he told his listeners. "It's time for the kingdom of God.

"Turn away from all your wrongdoing and believe the Good News."

Mark 1

Jesus knew he would need help to spread the message about God's kingdom. He chose twelve people to be his closest friends, the disciples.

The four fishermen

The first disciples Jesus called were men who fished for a living on Lake Galilee: Simon Peter and his brother Andrew, as well as James and his brother John. They left their nets to follow Jesus.

 Boats often worked in pairs to gather the catch in a dragnet. Each boat held one end of the net and they sailed closer together to trap fish.

A tax collector

One day in the marketplace Jesus saw a man named Matthew. He collected taxes for the Romans, and for that many people disliked him.

"Follow me," Jesus said to him.

Matthew got up at once. He invited Jesus to a feast along with many other tax collectors.

The rabbis who saw this sneered at Jesus' choice of followers.

"I have not come to call respectable people to repent of their wrongdoing," Jesus told them. "I have come for outcasts."

 Tax collectors used to set their stalls up in the markets while people came to shop.

Philip   Bartholomew   Thomas   Simon the Patriot (a freedom fighter)   James son of Alphaeus   Judas son of James   Judas Iscariot   Mary Magdalene   Susanna   Joanna

Seven more disciples

Jesus spent time praying before he chose the rest of his disciples.

Luke 6

Brave and loyal women

Women were also among Jesus' close followers. Some were wealthy and were able to help provide funds.

Luke 8

Jesus the Storyteller

When Jesus preached, he often told stories.

"Why do you do that?" his disciples wanted to know.

"The stories are parables," Jesus replied. "They have a hidden meaning that gives glimpses into what I mean by God's kingdom. Not everyone is going to understand them."

The parable of the sower

"Once," Jesus told his listeners, "a farmer went to sow seed in his field. Some fell on the path and birds ate it.

"Some fell on rocky ground. The plants sprouted but their roots did not go deep, and they withered.

"Some fell among bushes. The young plants that grew were choked.

"Some fell on good soil and produced a harvest."

Later he explained the meaning to his disciples:

"The seed on the path stands for those who simply hear my preaching. The Devil comes and snatches it away from them and they don't remember a thing I said.

"The seed on the rocky ground stands for those who hear my teaching and are eager to follow it. Then they find it harder than they thought and they give up.

"The seed that fell among bushes stands for those who try to follow my teaching but it never becomes truly important to them. Their busy lives get in the way of their becoming loyal followers.

"The seed that falls on good soil stands for those who hear my words and take them to heart. Their lives are good and fruitful."

Matthew 13

Seed was sown in a ploughed field by scattering. A plough was often used again to cover the seed with earth.

Ploughing and planting took place after the summer drought: from October/November to January.

Wheat and barley were harvested in April, May, and June. The stalks were cut with a sickle and tied into sheaves.

The sheaves were taken to the village's "threshing-floor", where the stalks were threshed either by hand with a stick or by using a threshing sledge – a board with bits of stone or iron fixed to it.

The loosened grain and broken stalks were then "winnowed" – tossed into the air so that the stalks blew away while the heavy grain fell back.

It was the task of the women of the household to grind grain into flour for breadmaking.

Stories About God's Kingdom

Jesus told stories about everyday things to explain what he meant by God's kingdom.

Matthew 13

The mustard seed

"God's kingdom is like this," he said. "A man sows a tiny seed. It grows into a huge tree, and all the birds come and nest in its branches."

dove
sparrow
raven
hoopoe

Yeast

"God's kingdom is like this: a woman takes a pinch of yeast and mixes it with a great bowlful of flour and water. The yeast begins to grow, and the whole batch of dough rises."

Hidden treasure

"God's kingdom is like this: a man is digging in a field when – crunch – his spade hits something. To his astonishment he finds he has struck a hoard of treasure.

"He fills in the hole and goes off to sell everything he owns so he can buy the field. When it is his, he comes to collect the treasure."

A perfect pearl

"God's kingdom is like this: a pearl merchant travels the world looking for pearls. One day, he discovers the finest pearl he has ever seen. He goes and sells all his other pearls so he can have the one that is perfect."

Weeds

"God's kingdom is like this: a man sowed a field of grain. One night, an enemy came and scattered weed seeds. Only when the crops grew tall did anyone notice. 'We must wait,' the man told his servants, 'until harvest. That will be the time to pull out the weeds and throw them on the fire. After that, we can gather the crops into my barn.'"

 Christians believe that, just as a seed must fall to the ground if it is to grow, so everyone must "die" before they can be part of God's kingdom.

Jesus the Teacher

When the crowds gathered to listen to Jesus, they would often stay all day. Here are some of the things he told them.

True happiness

"Happy are those who know they have lived their lives far away from God.
The kingdom of heaven belongs to them!

Happy are those who live as God wants;
God will make them his friends.
Happy are those who are kind and forgiving to others;
God will be kind and forgiving to them!"

Matthew 5

Flax was harvested in March and April. The plant was cut with a hoe near to the ground, and the stalks were dried in the sun on the houses' flat roofs. When dry, they were made into cord, nets, and linen cloth.

olive trees

flax

chamomile

hawk's beard

Going the extra mile

"Do not take revenge on anyone who wrongs you. Instead let them wrong you twice. If a Roman soldier asks you to carry his pack one mile, offer to carry it a second mile."

Matthew 5

Love your enemies

"You know the saying, 'Love your friends, hate your enemies.' I'm telling you something else: love your enemies and pray even for those who are unkind to you."

Matthew 5

True riches

"Don't wear yourself out trying to get rich. Neither money nor the things it can buy can keep you safe. Instead, do the things that please God, that build you a store of treasure in heaven."

Matthew 6

Seeking God's kingdom

"Do not be worried about the food you need to eat and the clothes you need to wear.

"Look at the wild birds. They don't spend their time sowing and harvesting, but God makes sure they have food to eat.

"And look at the meadow grasses. They don't spin yarn or stitch cloth. Even so, God clothes them in bright and beautiful petals.

"So make it your aim to be part of the kingdom of God and to live as God wants. You can be sure that God will provide you with all you need."

Matthew 6

date palms

corn poppies

Jesus' Words About Forgiving

Simon Peter once came to Jesus with a question.

"If someone has wronged me, how often do I need to forgive him? Seven times, perhaps?"

"Not seven," replied Jesus, "but seventy times seven."

He told Peter this story.

The unforgiving servant

"The kingdom of heaven is like this," said Jesus. "There was once a king who had lent money to his servants. He decided to check on how much.

"The first man he saw owed him millions. 'Unless you pay right now, I'll sell you as a slave,' roared the king. 'You and your family too.'

"The servant fell to his knees. He begged, he pleaded, he wept. The king felt quite moved and changed his mind.

"'Oh, forget the money. I can afford to let you off,' he said.

"As the man went back to his work, he saw a fellow servant who owed him money.

"'You scoundrel,' he roared, and he grabbed the man by the throat. 'Where's that money I lent you? I want it today.'

"The servant pleaded for more time, but the man shook his head.

"'Right – I'm sending you to jail,' he declared.

"When the king found out, he was furious.

"'I forgave you an enormous amount,' he said to the servant. 'You should have been as forgiving to others. Now you will suffer the punishment you gave the other man.'"

Matthew 18

Forgive others

Jesus said this: "If you forgive others the wrongs they have done to you, your Father in heaven will also forgive you."

Matthew 6

Jesus' listeners would have known how some of the local rulers lived. They would have remembered the bad days of Herod the Great.

Jesus' teaching about forgiving others was for everyone – even a servant with a master who treated him badly.

Jesus' Words About Repenting

To be part of God's kingdom, Jesus explained, a person had to live by God's standards. The first step was to repent: to admit to having done wrong and to want to make a new start.

"The people who think they're wonderful don't understand this," he said. "Humble people – even lowlifes – understand perfectly."

Rabbis were expert in the laws contained in the Scriptures. Many belonged to a group called the Pharisees. They were especially strict about tiny details of the Law... such as having long tassels on the shawls they used to cover their heads when praying.

Pharisee

tax collector

Temple priests

Two men in the Temple

"My story," said Jesus, "is about two men who went up to the Temple to pray. As the Pharisee entered the courtyard, he almost bumped into a tax collector.

"The Pharisee went straight to the front and made sure he was as far as possible from the cheating, conniving friend of the Romans. He stood tall and lifted his hands in prayer.

"'O God,' he began, 'I thank you that I am different from so many others. I am not greedy or dishonest. I am not a cheating husband. I keep all the religious rules, and you will have seen that I fast twice a week and give you a tenth of all I earn.'

"The tax collector stayed at the back of the courtyard and fell to his knees. 'O God, have mercy on me, a sinner,' he said.

"And do you know," said Jesus, "it was the tax collector who went home a friend of God."

Luke 18

coins in the time of Jesus

Zacchaeus

On one occasion Jesus went to Jericho. The local tax collector had been overcharging people for years and they hated him. They certainly weren't going to let him through to see the famous preacher. Zacchaeus climbed a tree to get a better view. Jesus saw him and invited himself to the rich man's house.

Zacchaeus was the chief tax collector in Jericho. He was too short to get a good view of Jesus, and the crowd wouldn't let him through, so he climbed a sycamore fig tree to get a better view.

Whatever Jesus said made Zacchaeus think hard about how he had overcharged people.

"I've decided," he told Jesus, "to pay back all that I've taken from people just to make myself wealthy. I'm going to pay back four times the amount."

Jesus was pleased. "This is what I came for," he said. "To call sinners to repent."

Luke 19

Jesus' Words About God's Forgiveness

Jesus' message was all about God. Even so, it was the very religious people who mistrusted him: the Pharisees and the rabbis.

"Just look at his followers!" they complained. "He treats wrongdoers and outcasts as his friends. He even shares meals with them."

Jesus replied with stories.

The lost sheep

"Imagine yourself as a shepherd. You have 100 sheep. Then one goes missing.

"At once you leave the 99 safely in the pasture and go and find your lost sheep. You are so pleased when you find it.

"God is like that shepherd, and I have come to call the ones who are lost back to God."

Luke 15

Sheepfolds were made of a stone wall in the shape of a ring with a gap as an entrance. When the sheep were safely inside, the shepherd would lie in the gap to sleep.

staff

sheepfold

broom

clay oil lamp

clay storage jars

The lost coin

"Think of a woman who has ten silver coins. One day she discovers one is missing.

"In dismay she lights a lamp so she can sweep her house carefully. She goes on looking until she finds her lost coin. She is thrilled when she finds it, and invites her friends round to celebrate.

"God is like that woman, and the angels sing for joy when someone who was lost is found."

Luke 15

29

Jesus' Story of the Lost Son

The rabbis and the Pharisees felt quite sure that they knew how to live in obedience to God. They looked down on those who failed in their duties.

Jesus told another story to show people how willing God is to forgive.

The lost son

"There was once a man who had two sons. The younger asked for his share of the family money so he could go and live life his way.

"In a faraway country he spent all he had. Times were hard. He needed a job – any job.

"That's how he ended up looking after pigs: underpaid, underfed… and deeply sorry about the mistakes he had made.

" 'I shall go home and ask to be a servant on my father's farm,' he sighed.

"As he came near to his old home, his father came running to welcome him, and threw a party.

"The other son was furious. 'Why does he get a party?' he demanded to know. 'I've been loyal and hard-working and get nothing.'

" 'Please come and join the celebrations,' said his father.

" 'You can be quite sure of this: everything I have is yours. Today, however, is not about you. Today is about your brother and we must be glad: because your brother, who was lost, has been found.' "

Luke 15

The younger son wasted all his money on fine living...

So when a famine hit the country he was in, he was left with no money.

Jesus' people, the Jews, thought that pigs were unclean. Looking after pigs was therefore the worst job they could imagine.

The father had been looking out over the long road, hoping for his son to return. He was overjoyed at seeing him.

The father demanded that his servants bring his son the best clothing and celebrate his return with a feast.

The elder son was so angry about the party that he refused to come in. His father went out to talk to him.

Jesus' Words About Prayer

Jesus often spent time praying. His disciples noticed he would get up early and go into the countryside to pray.

"It's enough that God sees you when you pray," Jesus told his listeners. "Don't stand up in the street where people can see you and admire you.

"You don't need to say a long prayer. Your Father in heaven already knows what you need."

Pharisees liked to make a big show of their praying by holding their hands high in public, wearing their long shawls with tassels, and wearing boxes containing passages of Scripture on their wrists.

Jesus gave his followers this prayer.

"Our Father in heaven:
May your holy name be honoured;
may your Kingdom come;
may your will be done on earth as it is in heaven.
Give us today the food we need.
Forgive us the wrongs we have done,
as we forgive the wrongs that others have done to us.
Do not bring us to hard testing,
but keep us safe from the Evil One."

Matthew 6, Luke 11

Ask, seek, knock

Jesus told his followers to be faithful in prayer and to trust in God, who is kinder than any human parent.

"Ask, and you will receive," he said. "Seek, and you will find. Knock and the door will be opened to you."

He told this story.

A friend at midnight

"Late one night you hear a knock at the door: a friend has arrived on a surprise visit.

"But, oh dear, you have no food in the house.

"You hurry to your neighbour to ask for some. You knock… and knock… and keep on knocking.

"At last you hear someone; 'Go away,' says an angry voice. 'We're all in bed.'

"But you don't give up. You really need to get some food for your friend.

"Even a grumpy neighbour will get up when you keep knocking. So you can trust that a loving God will answer your prayers."

Luke 11

33

Jesus' Words About Persistence

When Jesus spoke, many were eager to listen. Many said they would like to change their ways and be part of God's kingdom.

"If you mean that," Jesus said, "you need to be really determined. You will have to give up your old lifestyle. You will have to keep going even when things are tough.

"When a farmer starts to plough a field, he has a long job ahead. If you start ploughing your way as one of my followers, you have to keep going. Anyone who looks back isn't fit for the kingdom."

Luke 9

The tower

"Imagine," said Jesus, "that a man wants to build a tower. He needs to sit down and work out the cost. He needs to know if he has enough to finish the job.

"What will happen if he starts building and runs out of money halfway? Everyone will see. They will laugh and jeer and wag their fingers."

Luke 14

The bridesmaids

"No one knows when God will come to claim his kingdom," Jesus warned.

"There were once ten bridesmaids who had agreed to welcome the bridegroom to his wedding. Each had a lamp to light the way if it grew dark.

"It so happened that the bridegroom was later than expected. All the girls fell asleep. Their lamps burned low.

"Then came a shout: 'Here comes the bridegroom.' Five of the bridesmaids had extra oil. They refilled their lamps and the flames burned brightly as they walked beside the bridegroom into the house.

"Five had no more oil. They went to get more, but when they came back it was too late. The wedding party was in full swing… and they were locked out."

Matthew 25

Weddings took place in the evening. The bridegroom would be carried to the house by his friends, with the bride's attendants lighting the way with their oil lamps.

35

Who is the Greatest?

As Jesus grew more and more popular, the twelve disciples began to think more and more highly of themselves. In spite of all Jesus told them, they even began to argue among themselves as to who was the most important.

Jesus heard the quarrel. He took a child by the hand and went to deal with them.

"If you men want to be part of the kingdom, you are going to have to change and become like children. The greatest in the kingdom of heaven is the one who chooses to be humble. And whenever you welcome a child into the kingdom, you welcome me."

Matthew 18

Jesus welcomed children with open arms.

Jesus and the children

One day, some people brought their children to Jesus. They wanted him to say a blessing prayer for each of them.

The disciples turned them away. "He's too busy for children," they said.

Jesus came over to put them right. "Let the children come to me," he said. "Don't try to stop them. The kingdom of heaven belongs to such as these."

Matthew 19

Toys would have been made out of simple materials, like this wooden horse.

Two children playing the "mill game", which was a cross between noughts and crosses and draughts.

Ordinary servants

Jesus told a story to show his disciples what God expected of them.

"Suppose one of you has a servant who comes in from working on the farm. Do you tell him to relax over a nice meal?

"Of course not: you tell him to get your supper ready and then put on an apron and bring food and drink to your table. After that you let him eat.

"Does the servant get special thanks for all this? Of course not. And it is the same with you; when you have done all you have been told to do, say this:

"'We are ordinary servants; we have only done our duty.'"

Luke 17

Rich masters would have worn much finer and more colourful clothing than their servants.

Jesus Faces Questions

Jesus made it quite clear that even wrongdoers and outcasts would be welcome in God's kingdom. The Pharisees and the rabbis made it quite clear that they disagreed.

"That preacher Jesus!" they complained. "He doesn't seem to care about God's laws. He's leading people astray."

The sabbath

The Jewish people had rules about the seventh day – the sabbath. God's laws said it was a day of rest. When the religious leaders saw Jesus healing people on the sabbath, they complained.

Jesus explained that their teaching had made the law stricter than it really was. "What is the right thing to do on the sabbath: to save life, or to destroy it?" he asked.

Luke 6

The religious leaders were annoyed that Jesus healed people on the sabbath...

... and allowed his disciples to pick and eat grain, as it was against God's laws to do any work on that day.

Jesus responded that they wouldn't hesitate to save a sheep that had fallen into a pit on the sabbath, though that counts as work too.

Paying taxes

One day, the Pharisees tried to trick Jesus with a question about taxes. "We know you are honest and always tell the truth," they said. "Is it against our Jewish law to pay taxes to the Roman emperor?"

It was a trap. If Jesus said it was against Jewish law to pay taxes, they could accuse him of being a rebel. If he said no, they could accuse him of not knowing Jewish law.

Jesus asked for a coin. "Whose face and name are on it?" he asked.

"The emperor's," came the reply.

"There's your answer," said Jesus. "Pay the emperor what belongs to the emperor. Pay to God what belongs to God."

Mark 12

All Roman provinces had to pay tax to the emperor. The emperor at the time when Jesus was preaching was named Tiberius. Coins from that time include one bearing Tiberius's head.

The Most Important Law

One day, a rabbi came to Jesus with a question about God's law. He wanted to test if Jesus understood it properly.

"What is the greatest commandment?" he asked.

"What do you think?" Jesus replied. "What do the Scriptures say?"

"That's easy," said the rabbi. "We must love God with all our being, and we must love our neighbour as ourselves."

"Quite right," said Jesus.

The rabbi didn't want to leave it at that. "Who is my neighbour?" he asked. Jesus told a story.

The good Samaritan

"A man was going from Jerusalem to Jericho. On the way robbers sprang out, beat him up, stole all he had, and left him for dead.

"A Temple priest came by. He hurried on past.

"A helper from the Temple came by. He came to take a closer look before hurrying on by.

"A Samaritan came along. He stopped to help the man. He took him to an inn and made sure he was taken care of.

The road between Jerusalem and Jericho was rocky, and there were many caves in the hills around where robbers could hide.

Some robbers attacked the man, stripped him, and beat him up.

The man would surely die soon if someone didn't stop and help him.

"Now tell me," Jesus asked the rabbi. "Who was neighbour to the man?"

The rabbi felt awkward. The priest and the helper were good religious Jews. The Samaritan was a foreigner with different beliefs.

That was why he frowned as he gave his reply. "The one who was kind to him."

"Quite so," said Jesus. "Now you go and do the same."

Luke 10

The Samaritan gave two silver coins to the innkeeper. "Take care of him," he said, "and if you spend more, I will pay you back next time I come this way."

A priest who led the worship in the Temple came by. But he did not help the poor man.

A Levite, who was a helper in the Temple, even came closer to look, but was still not willing to help.

It was the Samaritan who acted like a neighbour and was the one to help.

Jesus the Healer

Jesus healed people. People might like his teaching or they might not; they could not dismiss the many stories of sick people being healed.

The hole in the roof

One day Jesus was preaching in Capernaum. People crowded into the house to listen to him.

Four men came along carrying a friend who could not walk. They each held a corner of his sleeping mat.

"We'll never get in the door," they agreed. "We're going to have to take desperate measures."

They went up the outdoor staircase to the flat roof. They broke through the mud plaster and let their friend down through the rafters on ropes – right to the feet of Jesus.

Jesus spoke to him with kind words. "Your sins are forgiven."

The rabbis looked angry and began to mutter. "That's so wrong! Only God can forgive sins. Who does Jesus think he is?"

Jesus knew what they were thinking. "Which is easier to say?" he asked. " 'Your sins are forgiven' or 'Get up and walk'? Now I want you to know that I have authority to forgive sins."

He turned to the man: "Get up, roll up your sleeping mat, and walk."

At once the man was healed. He did as Jesus said, and danced away.

Luke 5

Roofs were flat, and they were used for storing things and as a place to sleep on hot nights. Most houses had an outdoor staircase up to the roof.

The man born blind

One sabbath day when Jesus was walking along, he saw a man who had been born blind.

"Why can't he see?" the disciples asked. "Did he do something wrong, or is the fault that of his parents?"

"It's not to do with wrongdoing," said Jesus. "It is so we can see God's power at work."

He made a paste from mud and put it on the man's eyes and sent him to wash it off. When the man did this, he could see!

The Pharisees who heard the news were angry and confused. "How can the healing be from God?" they argued. "Jesus broke the law about the sabbath."

The man himself had only one thing to say. "Once I was blind. Now I can see."

John 9

The blind were just one group of people with a disability who were considered outcasts in Jesus' day; others included the lame, those with the disease leprosy, and those with deformities. Those unable to work may have had to support themselves by begging.

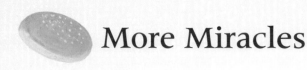

More Miracles

Jesus was not just a healer. He also worked other miracles.

Each was a sign that he had power from God – and a sign of just who he was.

Water into wine

Jesus and his disciples went to a wedding in Cana. Everything was going well – except that the host was running out of wine.

Jesus told the servants to fill some huge jars with water and then take a cupful to the man in charge.

When then man took a sip, he smiled. "Most people use up their good wine first and then move on to the cheap stuff," he said. "Here the best has been kept till last."

John 2

Storage jars like these would have been cut from a huge block of stone and turned on a lathe. They may well have had lids to keep dust and flies out.

At a Jewish wedding, the bride and groom sat under a special canopy while dancing and feasting went on around them.

The storm

After one very busy day, Jesus and his disciples got into a boat.

Jesus was so tired he fell asleep. Suddenly a storm blew up. The wind tore at the sail, and the waves tossed the fishing boat around.

"Wake up!" the disciples shouted to Jesus. "Come and help us, or we're sure to drown."

Jesus spoke to the wind. "Be still," he said. To the waves he said, "Lie down."

At once all was calm.

"Who is Jesus?" the disciples whispered. "Even the wind and waves obey him."

Mark 4

The Jews were not seafarers. In their storytelling tradition, storms stood for the dark forces of evil. This would have convinced the disciples that Jesus was the Son of God.

The great feast

One day, crowds of people gathered to listen to Jesus. They stayed for hours. Jesus noticed the sun sinking low. He spoke to his disciples. "You must give the people something to eat."

The only food in the crowd was what one boy had to offer: five loaves and two fish.

Jesus took them, said a thank-you prayer, and asked his disciples to share the food. There was enough for everyone.

John 6

When Jesus had finished giving out the food to the crowd, he asked his disciples to gather up the leftovers. To their astonishment, they could fill twelve baskets with all the leftover pieces of bread and fish.

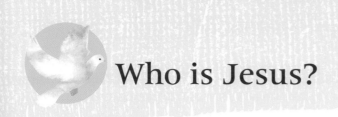

Who is Jesus?

Jesus became the talk of Galilee, and beyond.

One day, Jesus asked his disciples a question:

Who do people say that I am?

"Some think you are John the Baptist," they replied. "They know he has been beheaded. Criticizing the local king for wrongdoing was always going to be risky. When they see you, they say you're John brought back to life.

"Others say you're one of the great prophets of days gone by," they added. "Someone famous from the Scriptures."

"And you," said Jesus, "who do you say I am?"

Peter replied at once: "You are the messiah, the Son of the living God."

Matthew 16; Mark 8; Luke 9

shrine to Pan

Peter acknowledged Jesus to be the messiah in the city of Caesarea Philippi, north of Lake Galilee. Once known as Paneas, it was a place where people worshipped the Roman god Pan.

Many Jews longed to be free from Roman rule and hoped that one day God would choose them a king: the "anointed one" (in Hebrew, *mashiah* – "messiah"). God told the prophet Samuel to anoint first Saul and later David as king with olive oil ("anoint" means "smear or rub with oil").

The good shepherd

Jesus did not want his disciples to go around claiming that he was the messiah. He described himself in different ways.

"My followers are like my flock of sheep," he told people. "The only way into the safety of the sheepfold is through the gate, and I am that gate for my flock.

"They know my voice and they follow me.

"I am the good shepherd. I am not like the hired worker, who will run away if a wolf comes. If anything threatens my flock I will stay to take care of them. I will even die to save them."

John 10

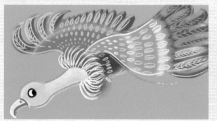 Sheep were kept in a sheepfold at night. The shepherd slept across the gateway to keep them safe from wild predators, which would have included:

vultures   bears   wolves

A Welcome for a King

For three years Jesus preached, told stories, and worked miracles.

As the time for another Passover festival came near, Jesus told his disciples he wanted to go to Jerusalem.

He asked them to fetch a donkey for him to ride, and then set out.

As he came near to the city, the crowds saw him.

They began to welcome him as if he were a king. They cut palm branches and waved them. They threw their cloaks on the ground to make a carpet for the donkey.

"God bless the king! Hooray for God's chosen king," they cried.

There were some Pharisees in the crowd and they were furious. "You mustn't let people think you're God's chosen king," they said. "Tell them to stop."

"It wouldn't do any good if I did," was all the reply they got.

Matthew 21, Luke 19

date palm branches

Pharisees

Roman soldiers

48

Many of the crowds seeing Jesus must have remembered the old Scriptures of their people and the prophecy in the book of Zechariah: God had promised to send them a king who would ride to Jerusalem on a donkey.

Enemies at the Temple

Jesus rode into Jerusalem and went to the Temple.

The festival market was in full swing. People were arguing noisily about money. Coins were jingling.

"This is all wrong!" said Jesus.

"The Temple is for prayer. You've made it a den of thieves."

He tipped up the market stalls and drove people out.

Matthew 21, Luke 19

A plot

The Temple priests and the rabbis met together. "We must put a stop to this Jesus affair," they said. "We don't trust his teaching, we don't approve of his lifestyle… and now he's letting everyone think he's the messiah.

"The problem is: how do we catch him without causing uproar among his followers?"

Matthew 26, John 11

A traitor

It so happened that one of Jesus' disciples had decided to betray his master. Judas Iscariot went to the priests with an offer: "If you pay me, I'll take you to Jesus when he's alone." The deal was done: for thirty pieces of silver.

Matthew 26

Some of the stalls were those of moneychangers, who exchanged coins for Temple money for the offering boxes. Others sold live animals, such as lambs and doves, to be offered at the Passover festival as sacrifices – giving something valuable to show that God was worth even more to them.

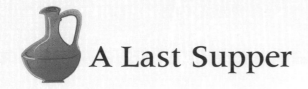

A Last Supper

Ever since he was a boy, Jesus had shared a Passover meal at festival time as the Jews remembered God's covenant of days gone by (see page 10).

"I've chosen a room in Jerusalem where we will meet this year," he told his disciples. "Please get everything ready."

A new commandment

Before the meal, Jesus tied a towel around his waist. "We haven't got a servant to wash your feet," he said. "So I'm going to be the servant."

When he had finished, he explained. "You must learn from this example – to serve one another humbly.

"This is a new commandment for you: love one another. That is how people will know you are my disciples."

John 13

The land Jesus lived in was hot and dusty. It was the custom for guests to have their feet washed on arrival by a servant.

It is possible that Jesus and his disciples would have eaten the festival meal in the Roman style, reclining on couches around a table.

Jesus breaks the bread.

Judas slips away.

Bread and wine

At the meal Jesus took the traditional bread, broke it, and shared it with his disciples.

"This is my body," he said, "broken for you. Remember to share a meal like this and remember me."

He also took the cup of wine and shared that around. "This cup is God's new covenant," he said. "It's a promise that will be signed with my blood."

As the disciples puzzled over Jesus' words, Judas Iscariot slipped away.

Luke 22

The ceremony Jesus carried out still happens when Christians meet as a church. It is often called Holy Communion and is a time to remember Jesus' words and God's promise.

✝ Crucified

Jesus and his eleven loyal disciples went out of the city to an olive grove called Gethsemane. They often went to this quiet place together.

Jesus knew what his enemies were planning. He spent time praying and asking God for help… until Judas came back, leading armed guards. Jesus let himself be arrested. The disciples fled.

On trial

The priests and religious leaders put Jesus on trial. It wasn't a fair trial: they had already made up their minds. They firmly believed that Jesus was disrespectful of God and God's laws. They wanted him dead.

Luke 22–23

Condemned

The priests did not have the right to pass the death sentence. They had to ask the Roman governor in Jerusalem to do that.

Pontius Pilate wasn't impressed. "I don't see that Jesus has done any crime," he said.

The priests had arranged for a mob to come and shout for Jesus to be crucified. Pilate didn't want trouble, so he agreed.

Jesus was crucified: nailed to a cross of wood until he died.

Luke 23

The crime

Every criminal had the name of their crime on a notice nailed above their heads. Pilate wrote it:

"Jesus of Nazareth: King of the Jews."

The priests complained. "He's not our king," they said. "You should have said, 'This man said…'

"Too late," said Pilate. "What I've written is what's going up in public."

John 19

Judas

When Judas saw what he had done, he felt guilty and ashamed. He went and hanged himself.

Matthew 27

The soldiers who were guarding Jesus mocked and beat him. He was brought before the chief priests and teachers of the Law.

Jesus was then taken to the Roman governor, Pontius Pilate, who asked him if he was king of the Jews. "So you say," Jesus replied.

After the soldiers crucified Jesus, they divided his clothes among themselves by throwing dice.

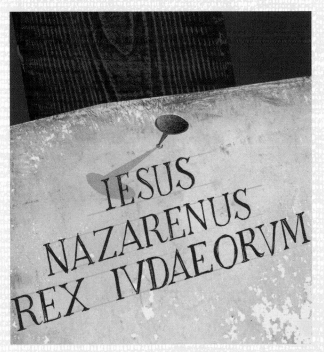

The notice Pilate wrote was in Latin (above), the official language of the Roman empire. It was also written in Hebrew and Greek.

On Sunday Morning

Jesus was put to death on a Friday. Friends came and took his body. They placed it in a stone tomb and rolled the door shut. Then they hurried away: the sun was setting and the sabbath day of rest was about to begin.

A wealthy man from Arimathea named Joseph was one of Jesus' followers. He got permission from Pontius Pilate to take Jesus' body for burial. He wrapped it in linen cloth and placed it in his own tomb.

Mary Magdalene

Joanna

Joseph of Arimathea

The empty tomb

Early on the Sunday morning some women came back to the tomb. They planned to wrap the body properly for its long decay.

To their amazement, the tomb was open... and the body was gone.

Angels spoke to them:

"Why are you looking among the dead for someone who is alive? Jesus is not here. God has raised him to life."

Luke 24

spices

Jewish people wrapped dead bodies in linen cloth and spices, including myrrh. Jesus' friends left his body on a shelf inside the tomb cave and slid a huge rock across the opening to close it.

folded linen cloth

Sometimes bones were placed in an ossuary (stone box).

57

Spreading the News

Over the next forty days, Jesus appeared to his disciples, often unexpectedly.

The couple from Emmaus

A couple who lived in nearby Emmaus met a fellow traveller on the way there from Jerusalem. They invited the stranger to stay the night. As he broke the bread at the supper table, they recognized him: it was Jesus!

Luke 24

Thomas

One day Jesus appeared to his disciples. But the one named Thomas was out at the time: he didn't believe what the others told him.

Later Jesus appeared to Thomas and showed him the marks on his hands and feet. Thomas stopped doubting when he saw Jesus.

John 20

The couple were surprised that the stranger said he hadn't heard the news about Jesus. The stranger told them, "Our Scriptures talk about how God's chosen one had to suffer. If Jesus was the chosen one, it had to happen that way."

Jesus said to Thomas, "Do you now believe because you see me? How happy are those who believe without seeing me!"

In Galilee

Peter was at a loss for what to do. The great adventure with Jesus seemed to be over.

"I'm going fishing," he said.

He and some of the others went back to Galilee. They fished all night but caught nothing. As they headed for shore, they saw someone waiting.

"It's Jesus!" cried Peter. He swam ashore.

As they shared breakfast over a charcoal fire, Jesus forgave Peter for not staying loyal on the arrest night. "I want you to take care of my flock of followers," he said.

John 21

A stranger on the shore told the fishermen where to cast – and the net was full! It was then that Peter recognized the stranger as Jesus.

The Good News

Jesus told his disciples he would not be on earth for long. "I must go back to God in heaven," he said. "I will prepare a place for you there.

"Now it is your job to spread the news about me and about God's kingdom."

Christians

With God's help, the disciples began to preach the news about Jesus.

"The man you crucified was a true descendant of King David," Peter told people. "He was God's chosen king – the messiah, the Christ."

"If you want to be part of God's kingdom, you must turn away from your sins and be baptized as followers of Jesus."

In Peter's day, many thousands became followers of Jesus Christ: Christians.

Acts 2

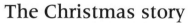

The Christmas story

Jesus' new followers wanted to know all about him.
His followers collected the stories of his life and teaching.
Among them were stories of his birth:

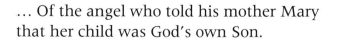

… Of the angel who told his mother Mary that her child was God's own Son.

… Of the baby born in Bethlehem – the birthplace of King David of old – and of the shepherds who came to see him.

Jesus told his disciples to make him known throughout the world. Peter first preached in Jerusalem and went on to travel to spread the news about Jesus. He also performed miracles; once, in the town of Joppa, he raised a woman called Tabitha to life.

"We saw angels," they told his mother. "They said we would find a baby in a manger just like this. They said he was the messiah, the one who will save our people."

… Of the wise men who followed a star to find the newborn king of the Jews: the star that led them to Jesus.

Glossary

angel   A messenger from God.

baptize/baptism   Christians baptize people who are new to the faith by dipping them in water. It is a sign that they want to follow God.

Bethlehem   A little town on a hill close to Jerusalem. King David and Jesus were both born here.

betray   To turn against someone.

Cana   A town in Galilee where Jesus performed his first miracle.

Canaan   The land where the people who became the Jews made their home.

Capernaum   A fishing village on the shore of Lake Galilee. Jesus moved there when the people of Nazareth rejected him as a teacher.

carpenter   Someone who makes things out of wood for a living.

Christ   A word derived from the Greek for "anointed". It means "chosen one", a king sent by God.

Christian   A believer in and follower of Jesus.

covenant   An agreement. God had several covenants with the people who became the Jews.

crucify/crucifixion   A Roman way of putting people to death by nailing or tying them to a large wooden cross.

David   One of the greatest kings in the history of the Jewish people. Joseph was a descendant of David.

Devil   The spirit of evil.

disciple   Someone who learns from a teacher. Jesus' special followers and friends were known as disciples.

festival   A time of celebration.

fisherman   Someone who catches fish for a living.

forgive/forgiveness   To stop feeling angry with someone about something they did.

frankincense   Gum from a tree, burned to make a sweet smell.

Galilee   The northern part of the country where Jesus lived. It had a big lake, Lake Galilee, where lots of fishermen worked.

Gethsemane   The garden where Jesus and his friends met the night before he died.

Herod the Great   A Jewish king who ruled on behalf of the Romans at the time when Jesus was born.

Holy Spirit   The invisible form of God, working in the world.

Jericho   A city about a day's walk from Jerusalem.

Jerusalem   The capital city in the land of the Jewish people.

Jews   The name of the nation who believed that God had chosen them to show God's love and mercy to the world.

John the Baptist   Jesus' cousin. He was a preacher in the wild country. He baptized people, including Jesus.

Joseph   The man to whom Mary, Jesus' mother, was promised in marriage. He was a carpenter.